Advance Praise for
Dylan Podson and *Vestiges of a Dark Night*

"Dylan Podson's poems are beautifully written, highly evocative, and deeply touching. His abundant compassion, sensitivity, and humanity are on full display in this remarkable collection."

Robert H. Deluty, Ph.D.
The Matter of Families: New and Selected Poems

"In this collection of poems, replete with images of darkness, struggle and near-death, Dylan generously brings us along on his journey with depression. He bravely confronts his demons, tracing the contours of his experiences and performing a kind-of alchemy with the results. This is not a book of answers; rather, it is a record of encounters, of honest confrontation with despair that finally reveals the miracle of life. Ultimately, these poems celebrate life, the miracle-in-the-mundanity of life, when a lovely day is one in which one is "alive and well" ("Deadmalls"). Threaded through the collection is always a glimpse, a sense, a whisper of hope."

Chinwe Edeani, Photographer

"These poems are a vulnerable glimpse into the mystery of the human condition. The writing hits you like a roaring river - scary and turbulent, yet deeply cleansing. Dylan's work is a powerful and uplifting cry for hope in these dark times."

Patrick Muhlberger, Filmmaker

Published by Endymion Press
Baltimore MD, United States of America

ISBN: 979-8-89546-900-2

First published globally, 2024

Vestiges of a Dark Night: Poems in the Pursuit of an Authentic Self
© Dylan Podson, 2024

Cover and interior design by Endymion Press
Fonts: Iowan Old Style, Adlery Pro, Adobe handwriting
Photos: All photographed and owned by the author.
Cover Photo: "Another Way Home," Gulfito, Costa Rica.

Section Title (Attributions):
"What Is Grief If Not Love Persevering?" (Laura Donney)
"The Best Criticism Of The Bad Is The Practice Of The Better"
(Fr. Richard Rohr)
"Life Is Not A Problem To Be Solved But A Reality To Be Experienced"
(Soren Kierkegaard)

Vestiges of a Dark Night:

Poems in the Pursuit of an Authentic Self

Dylan Podson

For Katie,
who's held onto the hope that life is beautiful.

"Sunrise," Kiruna, Sweden

As long as I fight, I am moved by hope;
and if I fight with hope, then I can wait.
~Paulo Freire~

Made weak by time and fate, but strong in will;
to strive, to seek, to find, and not to yield.
~Lord Alfred Tennyson~

All one can hope to do is to keep oneself humbly available,
to allow oneself to be a battlefield.
~Etty Hillesum~

Table of Contents

Introduction

"You know that you're disturbed, right?"

It's nearly Halloween 2011 as I sit up in my hospital bed to stare across a sterile room at the gaggle of white-coat doctors, trying to discern which of the lot just said this to my face. Confused by such brazen attempt at initiating a "medical" conversation, it takes seconds for it to sink in that I haven't quite had an easy go of it during this master's program at Tulane University. To some degree perhaps they were right, that the ways I viewed myself or handled relationships wasn't particularly healthy due to a slew of genetic and environmental circumstances. However, given such factors, I tended to perceive the world less rose-tinted than others and had developed a blunt pragmatism that allowed me to not only persevere but thrive throughout so much of life's most challenging seasons.

If we could pivot slightly for a moment to an interest of mine, that of professional wrestling, I think it could help explain why any of this matters. See, in that world there exists a terminology called "kayfabe" which means performers are to strictly keep up the theatrical illusion where what happens inside the ring is really happening. It means that what you see is what you get such that storylines and characters are all true to life as presented. This creates excellent performances for the audience in a show where every aspect is believably intriguing and doesn't break the magic.

The reason I bring all of this up is because I see so much consistency with keeping "kayfabe" and how our society behaves publicly, especially when it comes to our presentation around others. We're raised from young ages to project a version of ourselves which fits into agreeable characters, neat packages and pleasing stories. In other words, it's a level of conforming (i.e., acting) to a role which won't rock the proverbial boat or impede other's expectations of us. Surely, each of us has heard it said from playgrounds or the office to "just go with the flow," "don't be selfish," "you're being weird," "she's so negative," or "he's too emotional." Whether we've formally agreed to it or not, William Shakespeare was on to something when he said "all the world's a stage, and all the men and women merely players."

As much as I love good drama, I've learned along the way that our personal lives deserve a much higher standard of authenticity and accurate representation. I'd commit to saying that this is especially true when it comes to our expression of things like unmet needs, daily anxieties, or untreated trauma. It has gotten to the point that individuals from every generation across society have forgotten what it looks like to ask for help, share a private concern or to "break character" for their own general benefit. You wouldn't need me to list statistics on the mental health crisis in this country given that it's already on the nightly news and emerging from our public spaces where discussions on our personal identity, community resilience, and coping mechanisms are frequently touched upon. Clearly, a bulk of us is shouldering a "burden to perform," but what would it look like to reverse these unnatural trends and in what manner could we proudly rediscover our unique voice?

This gathering of eclectic poems was meant to simply be my participation in breaking "kayfabe," that is, working through what it is to be fully and unapologetically human. Topics covered run the gamut of such life-long experiences from heartache and loss to love and the sublime. Imagine it as an attempt to freely embrace and communicate that which makes life worth living – exalted virtues such as hope, curiosity, introspection, and perseverance through suffering. Together, with each of us expressing our truths through self-validation, we can uncover an inner strength both dynamically flexible and communally durable.

As someone once labeled "disturbed" with their fair share of mental health diagnoses and who struggled with self-acceptance, I've wrestled with what it means to work toward outspoken authenticity. Sometimes the way forward looks subtle

 ❖ *Vestiges of a Dark Night*

and graceful; other times it's an unexpected breakdown on a disappointing road. So, whether you're making first steps on this reflective journey or are a seasoned veteran of life's highs and lows, take what you will from these words of mine and make it fearlessly yours in any way you can. My hope is that you may be inspired to express your own true self and leave everything else to the wayside. Go in peace.

Dylan Podson
August 2023

988 Suicide and Crisis Lifeline

If you or someone you know is experiencing a mental health, suicide, or substance use crisis or emotional distress, reach out 24/7 to the 988 Suicide and Crisis Lifeline by dialing or texting 988 or using chat services at suicidepreventionlifeline.org to connect to a trained crisis counselor.

"Less Traveled," Colchuck Lake, WA

I.

Lost & Found,

or

What Is Grief If Not Love Persevering?

Seconds Go

I wish to see your smile
wide as cheeks allow
so our laughter might crash with
the stargazers who soak in the rain.

A melody so sweet and pure,
your voice an ancient chord
striking every note of this autumnal hymn.

Warm and radiant,
your eyes an eclipse
with their upkeep of hues.

Cobblestone slaps wet underfoot
as silhouettes dance
from post to fiery post.

Give It A Chance

The sky hangs overhead
like drapery to a window
just out of reach.
Life on one's toes can burn out sinew
but only dreamers know.
A tree whispers gossip in the day's breeze
and for just one moment
time is suspended for directional change.

The love is here.
Fear is gone.
The words are beauty.
Truth is power.

Peace exists and I can feel them now;
all my muscles exuding
white-hot banners which flutter freely.

<h1>Resurrection</h1>

The beauty in how she lives her life
astounds even the spring flowers,
working extra shifts in this late winter
to play catch up.

Core pounds to the beat of
another foreign country
yet one glance to realize she is not.
Borders may restrain her by birth,
fortunate love is not held captive by topography.

It flows beyond zones of security
and escapes every limit
which was once imposed.
She is but one crusader
out of a histrionic mission field
and into the real one.
No encapsulated experience or
erroneous expectation.

Simply
one heart,
one woman;
her tears shed
for both Cairo and campus.

Child's Play

Beside me,
a hidden box of shiny toys.
Out of view or thought,
gathering strength to cry for attention.
They mustn't be found -
what poor intentions to share.

A simple trick:
denial of platform and voice.

Nothing at all.
Merely temporary housing
'til I find the right use
other than what they beg for.
Such silly little toys.

Up & Away

Thoughts rush toward the ceiling,
a wave of hot steam.
Boiling, it stirs and stirs.
Questions dash against the spine and
her soul is on fire.
The sensation is one of passion,
a thing of rarity existent in the yellowed margins
of some old romantic's ledger.

Frequently,
lesser scribes tried to fill time
with toils and plunders
but chemicals catalyze into emotion
bearing no price or limitation.

Radiant,
they tear through the haze
caused by all of this mind's pollution
and rise further still –
the stars so pure and splendid.

A thing of childhood fantasy,
lazy summer evenings which sing on and on.
The slow melody tunes to heartstrings
and courts that hunger unlike
any sweet condolence could do.
Steadily, it carries along still waters
and through green pastures
like a pleasant whisper calling her name.

It is a title written on the pages of time,
one known by the infinite
still a blessing to the temporal.

Love descends
and carves her from the same source,
a fount of beauty.
This life she has known
is but self-proclaimed mystery,
however,
to the world
it is nothing short of a miracle.

Pounding Mannerisms

Endless praises sit.
Stagnant are the forgotten.
Unspoken joys drown.

Memories of her,
lay fresh like fallen snow.
Yet when will it return?
Her melting shape.

Tired gods grip hard
to the red gate at my arms,
but still it boils fast and deep.

Slow Count

I wouldn't have to feel much,
just light from the innkeeper
signaling a final end
of the long night's ride
through storms deep raging.

Heaven and hell
battling for dominance
over my weary carriage,
broken rider and all.
Soon they shall know,
but what suspense
drills this space 'til it's out!

Ears widening to pray they
be filled like the gorge of my heart,
not with the crack of a stake
but immaculate psalms
to venture on home.

Repercussions

White-hot lightning courses throughout my body,
half-expecting to see limbs aflame
with this burnt searing.
But there they lay,
quiet and still,
hidden ocean of endless disruption
tumults just below a silky surface.

I imagine veins will be crawling
like worms at the top of my soil
to rear their neon head in
one thousand intricate networks,
but again, I'm pristine as an obelisk;
towering misrepresentation
of the beams injecting pain
throughout every pore.

Blink
and you'd miss my lower half escape without me,
my limbs detach to slowly orbit
around my head in a jester's halo.

The Walking Wounded

Over the centuries there has undoubtedly
been countless dead-men-walking.

A man sentenced to the gallows has but a handful of nights
to embrace any nostalgia from his past.

A convict on the run has exhausted every last safe house
and hears the jowls of encroaching hounds.

A child rides back from the hospital while his parents
struggle to focus on the blurred road, diagnosis in hand.

A martyr takes one last leap of fate and
condemns himself in a hostile land of misdirected ignorance.

Live beyond such likened finale
where violence finds men in their depths.
To transition beyond the swaying noose,
having accepted the death-like beauty of rebirth itself.

Companionship

In the mall tonight,
I'll keep my eyes peeled
for Fyodor, for Leo, and for Sylvia.

Two out-gambled, sickly men
with a needy, feverish look about them
yet with minds which can
piece together the unimaginable depths
of passer-byers' souls.

And she,
wounded and overlooked Jane
with meek demeanor but powerful spirit
who's too busy shattering patriarchal ceilings
to find herself in love,
sidetracked by critiquing ways
in which it's clear
she's most unwelcome in those spaces.

Time moves by faster now
and I'm left with these pages in hand,
ghostly relics screaming
at the top of their lungs to wake me up.

Llorando

Part I

Slipping into the closet, attraction futile to fight.
The stars are gone, all glowing ceased.
Struggle, quicksand takes everything.
Empty rooms with thrashing papers,
texts from a newfound perforation.
It isn't found, the space which has taken,
now is isolated given what's granted.
Time flies where his absence reigns,
funny how perfect attendance was ever a goal.
Today it's broken forever and nobody'll know.

Part II

This free weekend is smooth enough;
far worse is the first few days of lost work.
Does the dirty phone ring in fear,
changing from what's expected to a worst case?
The cold leukemia laughs,
a boy bestowed with love alone walking small.
My closet carrying brighter secrets,
one cry and the slipping-void swallows whole.
Unable to ask for flowers,
wry as the empty tomb,
no further evidence left to scar.

Hello Old Friend

Ingested tomb,
buried in the depths and then gone.

You are the white slab,
missing dates to confuse.
Why so planted yet held in trepidation,
half-chiseled sobriety?

I've traded crawfish for crabs,
but you were never far.
Displacement,
relocation expenses paid for
by soaring premiums and shellfish coverage.

All The Things She Said

This, the unforgettable sin,
a tattoo unrequested, forever changed.
No shrew flesh, no fashionably guilty yearbook photos.
No lifelong partner resounding with Hollywood fervor.
Cannes endures bitter disappointment.

Flex the sand,
watch it slip between your fingers
as it did before.

Defunct,
to the debts I owe,
escaped such roulette for another day.

Wait your turn,
I'd suggest meditation.
Three years and seven months is too long,
but I'm hoping for certain
that you always get the chance
to fight these headstones just a little while longer.

Concierge Services

Bellhop's rack down a long hallway,
headed toward most quiet destination.
Solace is sought,
if only for the night.
It never comes.

A boy choking in size 12 shoes,
with salary to match.
But this smolder never
draws attention to his needs.

Guests oblivious,
sharing that much with the family.
Unaware of the thick smoke
consuming everything.
He carries bumbling bags,
begging for it to end.

One shoe falls.

The needle skips,
judging eight-ball quivers.
Storm's eye never even appeared,
flowers full of deceit and false pretense.

Authority strikes.
Whip crack
of bolts clear across a night sky.
Never known how far its slice fractures,
his past cleaving-out entire segments of my future.

Diving Off Pier 6

Swaying, mostly silent.
A million distractions egg me on.
The drugs, the women, the high.
Much of it manufactured and fake,
even more easy-going trouble.

Yet I'll deny their futures
and find myself in a different tide.
I'm rolling, carried to the pier's edge.
City lights all around, I'm engulfed
but by too much.

Can I breathe for one moment
and escape its sound,
the cacophony?
I fight to know whether
I'm made for more than this precarious ledge.

Drifting to heart,
born for this dance.
Come home.
Finally,
I'm coming home.

Forty-Five

I say he's dead.
Corporate horn with matching deluxe edition
complete with spineless business card and
signature leather belt-buckle crack.
Still his empire lives on
beyond the grave
like the seedy florescent lights
of a wheezing casino strip.
Forgotten, its heyday was decades past,
relic of a bygone era when the breadwinner
dominated households like a boardroom,
executive fist-in-tow.

I'd like for it to disappear from my heart
but still he remains like smoke exhaled,
clinging to curtains, staining our simple 60s rancher
built by strong hands, hard work, and the American dream.
Cut short like my jerk on a steel beam,
short like the pink tiles mocking my iron wrists.
Everything left praying
I wouldn't have to be so young and tragic.

Happy Halloween

Countless tubes pierce through
to carry desperate fluids toward my weakened cause;
a context the human body
doesn't typically find itself in,
needing to be flushed or purged.
Tried to bleed out like some leeches
the medieval physicians once used –
similar chance for success.

I'm ripped from intentions
with a violent shake
and the whiplash has me reeling.
Restrained from myself,
course now changed forever,
I am not to be trusted with independent capacities.
I never should've been
but there are ways to feign authenticity,
a virtual reality to hide
these horrific stagehand strings.

Curtains pulled back
where gears get set in motion by absent hands,
revealed to parents like lesser gods.
Still, clumsy participation is required ahead.

I can almost hear them
now calling to come drown
but I've a race to win;
I'd always heard I wasn't done,
now I've seen I never will be.

Inside Your Neighborhood Pharmacy

The night is cool and crisp,
she's already got me wanting to jump
into leafy piles
or make snow angels,
simply twirl with my arms
in the middle of the street.

A kid again,
embarrassed for the half-dozen things I've done,
less so for a dozen more I haven't yet.

Deadmalls

Driving to the mall on a lovely day
(I imagine it was because I was alive and well),
turn into what is known as a consumer's safe haven.
For the rest at least.
This destination somewhat more morose for myself
and every terrified yet determined intention I harbor.

Hardware aisle purchase,
I place a cheap price on my soul
and bother not to whimper my plan to the cashier
for fear they'd stop me.
The world's a crazy place after all
and who knows what a person would do.

In my 1970s bathroom,
safe and sound,
the pink tiles are framed
and quietly gazing on with a visceral intent –
proximate masculinity but nary a trace of a father
to warn, protect, or hold.

No,
just a few moments of
tremendous anticipation
before a pendulum's swing;
I'm already a success yet can barely manage to balance,
all to Poe's delight.

Say It Again

I am stronger than you, after all,
you black mass of deceitful folklore from yesteryear.
I always was, before my genetics formulated
their plan against me and
my stomach grew sturdy to outlast.
You fought for years to bury this certainty
like the light inside you've buried underground.
Crippling fear of your own reaper,
silent hooded executioner,
has disfigured features of your soul
and now you fight to extinguish mine.

I am too bright a being to face
so you've lost everything in life to count as gain against me.
But 6 feet is a laughable distance for such radiance
and no battery could ever dim the one true story I know,
the one that I'll tell, that I'll live-out.

How, you feebly ask?
By outlasting you.

Or perhaps by rearing lights of mine own
who'll populate and change the world
one cold misanthrope at a time.
We'll dedicate time to the widows, orphans and destitute
without fueling our reserves through hypocritical bloodshed
        at home.
Indeed, I am an ever-evolving flurry of strength and hope,
        bravery and faith –
concepts foreign to your base.

I'm alive and in love with every breath;
dearest,
oh dear,
you bastard,
I'm through with you.

Checkmate

Time moves on
and every moment is lost to the waves,
fellow travelers which eat and spew,
regurgitating a constant that cannot be stopped.

She exits the room
because my shine is too far dim
but if she cannot stomach a minute of my high,
how am I supposed to endure the ever-present lows?

Perhaps it shows her hand,
reveals how much strength
she's unwilling to consider skin in the game.

The Used

Steel and iron-tinged kiss of death,
cold and solid, the weight intensifies.
But I also think of you.

Barrel strong enough for jaws,
mine burst in aching tension.
And still, I think of you.

Tracing outlines like my neighboring Greeks,
I'll connect the dots with one try and slide.
So how else can I think of you?

Effortless
and I splash amongst the stars,
joining Hollywood should've never been this easy.
I look up and think of you.

Deprived of moments to regret
I lose years.
With the rest to come, who drew a straw so short?
Life amid the chambers' maze
because of all these thoughts of you.

Providence

Back in the house are scraps of memories.
Quilted together,
we stay up playing dress rehearsal.
The new dog has replaced me,
he's got growing pains to endure.
Flannel blankets protect them from the stillness –
I opt out and slink down the stairs.

1790s, 1850s, they crowd me on either side.
Stories flow across and mix with mine.
We are intimate tonight,
the bored ghosts and I.
Silence carries a weightless moan –
I'm caught reeling yet intrigued.

Horsemen jeer from the shadows,
my tight scarf and I.
"Love me, I was meant for you."
The only thing that changes are the echoing footsteps,
headed briskly toward whatever new realization I pray.
Can these cobblestones speak like God?
Would a lingering car snatch me from these hills like loose
        change?
I kick brown leaves,
my nostrils open wide.
"Save yourself."

The games remain inside and I'm out buying paper.
Perhaps that was just a walk with the cherries,
still it changed my life like I want this street to tonight.

Dylan Podson   43

Gimme A Break

Gasping for air, I emerge from Sheol, everything
is bright-white starbursts as the precious fuel fills my lungs.

This is what's at the eye of the storm, a singular moment
to gather your thoughts and evaluate what does or does not
      work.

Intentional, deliberate, I seek greater control over my
thoughts in order to emote my way through healthier
      pastures.

I want to predict the future just enough that, no matter the
      outcome,
I'm in some sense prepared and in-tune with my self
      trajectory.

So, whether it's the calendar days I allow to premeditate, or the
slightly-detached delivery of said confessions, I'm taking
      charge of it all.

Dubrovnik

All the wars lined up along the coast,
edging against the blue-green Adriatic.
Misery, crimes to humanity at its wake,
even the miraculous is exposed as vulnerable.
Comforted under the tanned orange,
pray tonight for the salvation of marbled clay.
Justice hides beneath innocent exterior,
destinies of those enslaved cry out.
Waves crash on bone, 'gulls caw in mourning,
the soil itself recognizes our flawed designs.

Later, roads and attractions rebuild in time,
as those who remember hold memories
of seaside horror.

"Spring's Snow," Leavenworth, WA

II.

Sinner & Saint,

or

The Best Criticism Of The Bad Is The Practice Of The Better

Siavonga

Exuberance in these lakeside sunsets,
still I see slow late-night rides.

Unexplainable beauty in clear blue skies,
and now, we're at brunch together.

Thousands of miles with hours into the bush,
yet my thoughts trace back to you.

A world at increasingly-capable fingertips,
but I'd swim the Atlantic for us.

On The Lower Zambezi

There exists such a thing called inertia
which doesn't take kindly to
an outside force changing the state it's residing in.

The world is full of it and
quite simply refuses to be told differently,
much like a spoiled toddler.

It holds a set course,
one which all of us regularly contribute to mind you,
and will fight a most unfair fight to maintain
any semblance of persistency.

So, what else could I expect from the way of things
as I enter the picture with an
air of curiosity, of humility, of compassionate sensitivity?

One royal dictate from a queen:
the world can't love you when you're changing it.

 Vestiges of a Dark Night

Holland

A vast network of canals
orchestrate the silent,
geometric backdrop to this idyllic town.
Weeping willows drift aimlessly
with the wind under overcast skies,
lowering their vivid arms
to gently dip into waterway avenues.
Wooden boats anchored along
the sides bob peacefully amidst a myriad of
lean architectural gifts from centuries past.

This city makes one want
to dance, to toss the phone, to chase
endless brick-lined streets throughout the night,
to taste the romantic kiss of history.
Respond to its calming air
and bike until you hear the music encroach itself
thru to the secrets of your heart.

Out Of The Darkness

Prior October nights lay before
my feet like a plowed field with fruitful gain.
Growth happened here,
surrounded by the sounds of
gently-lapping waves and seagulls' caw.
At dusk I've sat on cold concrete stoops,
watching tears splash into a darkened bay,
connecting with an infinite wisdom
where spirit is a more suited listener
than I could ever be.

All that tragedy, hurt, longing
left alone and silenced:
did it burn off with the dimly-lit candles
drifting past the harbor in slow currents,
or was it carried through the night sky on a sweet breeze?

I knew comfort in those moments,
in a brief respite.
More assured than ever that
not only was I existing in a community
of strength and love,
but how I'd been blessedly cared for
by a greater cosmos – shepherd staff and valley too.

Not Everything Is Evil

Like guests stacked for miles
arriving at a grand ball,
I stand watch at the door
and attentively welcome each one.
I face this endless line
regardless of the humanity deck
which appears to shuffle
and replace itself front to back,
acknowledging each one
as it passes by and leaves me yet again,
still waiting for a chance to return.

Some guests stay briefly
and warmly engage with me.
Others demand my immediate and
sustained attention,
while more appear so similar to
one another that I'm sure the repetition
is beginning to numb
my ability to distinguish between.

No matter.
I hold inner peace along the frame
and maintain a greeter's passing place
along this riverside
to be softly carried off.
Away to the here and now,
away to my blissful presence.

Zhaolin Park

Subzero degrees
with my back up against
the firm tree trunk,
blanketed by night
on every side yet
faintly illuminated with carnival lights.
Everything is fine here in the snow
and I fret nothing outside this
pure capsule because I know that
I am enough.

Deep-breathing through my nose
with a clarity unbeknownst for years,
I find myself striding passionately
down the wide boulevard with confidence.
I feel carefree and majestic,
nonchalance a mile high.
Stepping purposefully into
a drifting column of smoky sulfur,
I ingest every bit of its streaky soot.

Simultaneously, I fully sense
the sporadic pops of brightly-lit lanterns
shooting life into the new year
as a suppressant to turn away
all the misguided ghosts of our mind.

Homecoming

Just last week I was walking through
the darkened halls of an ancient castle
and stuck around for a few minutes longer,
allowing a song's instrumentation ample opportunity
to stir something in my habitually-hurried heart.

Almost like unexpected clockwork,
goosebumps swell along my skin and
group together at the precise moment
that a euphoric jig erupts into the chorus.
I submit my body and soul to fully comply
and step out of the stone's dank shadows.

Engulfed by the courtyard's warmth
and smiling effortlessly in the sun,
I know I haven't telegraphed a single emotion here
but rather provided the moment to settle
so that divine essence could share
a bit of its love for me;
the love I've run from,
abandoned countless times
in-between pursuits of an overactive mind,
a broken heart and weary childhood -
still, I'll always remember this dance.

Talking About Practice

Climbing into the stratosphere overlooking
lush fields of Olympic-pace obstacles.

Creaking pines atop bleachers tinning.

Beach seats yield wide views of adoration,
a rose and chocolate hearts wait hiding inside.

Creaking pines atop bleachers tinning.

Girls wield power in plays of net and sticks,
boys praying eternity begins with one last whistle.

Between Here And Bogota

Slightly buoyed,
my ankles dangle over the lip of the board,
hoisted with enough clear-blue mystery
to keep the tip of my nose and pursed lips dry.
Like tiny islands, I'm out drifting among the kelp and crabs.
Ears get replaced with new sensations
and my steadied breathing becomes all-encompassing,
I resist the cresting urge to panic
and instead focus on a pristine weightlessness.
Cooly comforted, my thoughts try to scatter in buckshot
but there isn't enough room to be distracted by much else
and the only thing that enters into this moment is a mindful
        presence.

Now with limbs lifted near the dockside,
I place a visor over my glasses and lay back,
arms outstretched along the paddle
to express solemn impressions of the Christ.
I could wander like this forever,
reddened shirtless,
completely disconnected and without concern for place or
        time.
I abandon all expectations and lose control of
the world whispering demands to my heart.

Contemplation

I have come so very far.
And yet, I am here at the beginning.
The wondrous thing is how
I get to decide whether such statement
be discouragement or praise.

The cliché in nature is a beautiful thing.
Crunching leaves. Cawing birds.
A tender, endless whispering wind
speaking through the soon-barren treetops.

Slow. Slower now.
Slowing in toward absolute stillness.
Be still and know the silence.
Love is the silence speaking
my name back to me kindly.
The eyes to see, ears to hear.

Stillness is the only move worth taking.
No other result but peace in the quiet place.
Not from across the ocean,
its masses of men,
with the pressure maintained within you.

I wait in the silence,
to be silent for you here.
Listening, you speak out to me
as the earnest universe
where deep calls to deep.

Nerves, anxiety, tension,
and desperation exist as an act of futility.
The answers aren't conquered through battle
or defeated in war.
It is the release of control,
the current of the river,
the swaying of the reeds with each tide.

Acceptance. Allowance.
A resignation to love.
Dreams of dancing in the dark.
Who am I, ask the stones.
Deeper than this body.

The Problem With Pain

…Yet amidst that disorientating place of dim confusion,
something like a flicker of energy or moment of laughter
reminds me that perhaps life isn't so far from us after all.
Spontaneous convulsions as I dance across the house,
a sweaty high-kick to the sky,
a frigid drive home where the highway's racing soundtrack
      cracks
just enough to yearn alongside ancestral screams.

More subtle?
What about the sneaking suspicion
or dawning realization that perhaps the most uncomfortable
      thing,
radical acceptance through being mindful with the power of
      now,
is ever-so possibly present as the very salvific rescue we've
      been longing for –
what else are we to do with our pain but craft endless
      religions?

Holding On

Thrashing about with windmill grace to punk,
screaming that if there's anyone out there,
they'll give me a sign.

Lungs expand then contract to match my elevation
past lofted history, beaming into view.
The best moments of my fleeting life
are witnessing hidden glasses sail across the room
and stripping this wounded façade of its liminal tenure.

Left wildly succumbing to the dancefloor's tenderness,
prostrating comfort received in experiencing
how much this broken-yet-giddy bow really matters.

This feeling, so far from the systematic mountaintops
which shook my soul with imposing dogma,
freely gifted as a symbol of molecular vibrations –
it produces sudden volcanic flare-ups
of hope-connected wellsprings in my presence.

Abide in me,
forestry of delight,
rest in me!

Bagpipes Over Miami

Like all the rest,
I lost my childhood
a long time ago.

Flush with a confluence of cosmic rates,
this lockbox feeds on flesh.

Visceral tragedy in its wake,
I've cried over countless coffins,
each one smiling up at me and eyeing a tense handle.
Trust the gap and leap over local streams,
I'll remember it as the day
I nearly drowned that concussed man.
What a tale to tell!

An introduction to shame comes harsh at first,
but we all get used to how calories nourish in the long run.
Strap-in faith played a role
until I found the words simply couldn't rhyme –
who'd believe science failed
at fitting into formulaic prose.
So, I promised my words always would,
despite the puzzled discordance indicating otherwise.

"Father" isn't accurate,
I may have misplaced the instructions forced upon me
with which I ran marathons by.
I eventually lost him too,
from the same seaside as churchyards swallowed me whole.

Wooden cross in the corner
was the carpeted cot of cotton swabs,
but militant service scared me to death.

Through the humiliation,
I'd loved him for years
as the principalities demanded tests
from privately prayerful indication
of a road I barely limped along.

Wholly collapsed,
the trinity stood between me
and a drained hospital bed,
while invasive flames disbanded lingering bacterial disease.

I know you never had one,
child,
so here I am.

Rest In You, Resting In Me

Taking off at a sprint,
dropping the cup in the running sink
with its orchestral cascades wasting.
A full-tilt burst of kinetic energy
traveling across the Persian plains of faith,
sighting the waning day's everglow
between two massive gateway columns.
Enchanting an orange haze around this slingshot
whereupon it came from sizzling purple tears
and into a grandiose throne room
complete with majestic,
near-dizzying heights held aloft.

The newfound cavern allots grace with each drawn breath
and silently-sacred replies.
I've snared tips over galley-floorboards escaping
the darkness' heavy gravity.

Greater gaps increasingly form beneath my soles
and nevertheless persist under accommodating beams
in rotation
spinning once-foreboding tales of terrific deceit.

It's where I find my homecoming flight
after the Hughesian jailbreak from doubtful conformity.
The entirety of the atmosphere cackles
for the completed journey,
its origins being dropped off
by some saint's canal
with merely a trick-or-treat bag in hand.

Here, I am true to both my cloudy foreign mountains
and local moonshine hollers,
such that everything I'll ever need
exists within my wellspring:
a joyous hope without expectation
of bearing pristine fruit.

All shall be well
for this pump rejuvenating life into veins
that were once forlorn of what universal mystery
causes the ever-persistent possibilities
to sail forever home in my heart.

Across Campus

She eventually caught up with me after class,
my head nestled between
the elegant and faceless tombstones.
I'd slept through Summer break and
spent my very own Halloween celebration among the mossy
      dirt.
This house I ran from no longer gripped me with fear,
hidden away,
as I was fully vulnerable here in wooded cocoon.
A restoration taking place
amid potent reminders of our oft-trampled
yet ever-inviting openness to truth.
I'm dying too, she said,
and I sheepishly wave over for her warmth
to come join my contented tears in gaze of the crashing
      moon.

Goodnight Oblivion

Proud to carry the courage required to stand
on such shaky and unstable edges.

Fullness of a desire to experience
resigned acceptance amidst empty frustration.

Where these same shouts over an abyss
are our very exit from despair.

You & Me

You,
Grandiose Condition,
saved my life and accompanied me for so long that I've
      forgotten
who I truly am sans the clinging, residual fears of oft-echoed
      anxious uncertainty.

You,
Deteriorating Mystery,
first gave me the fire to burn out brighter than any could've
      ever imagined
and harbored such infinite depths of clawing persistence.

You,
Saintly Curse,
carried since youth, where "home" was to be punished, on
      thru to the oversized
ICU scrubs which were initiated as the only companions to
      guard me at night.

You,
Outdated Guardian,
centered upon the prolonged battles aimed to take us both
      away from
free consciousness, regardless of how I've since urged your
      relieved distance.

But I,
Aged Survivor,
pray in strength to formed and formless Being that your
        teeth depart from me.

I,
Graceful Purpose,
seek a joy you cannot provide nor reside over.

I,
Compassionate Forgiveness,
bid you a fond farewell and well-deserved final rest.

I,
Beloved Contemplative,
am powerfully safe in the present moment's here and now.

Godspeed,
Blessed Gift,
for my life has just begun to run free from pain and
into the arms of my ever-accepting self.

Halmstad

In the pinkish reflection of the LED dream-towers,
I now know it all.

In the longest shadow of their thick, dueling plumes,
I know everything.

In the Nordic seaside town's chilly tundra,
I know far too much than what I arrived with.

Western Ways Of Cold Violence

I've heard it described
I'm the sand slipping through fingers
and how with every new burst of commitment,
she comes away losing novel pieces of me.

I've held prayerful hands,
stained by endless tears
and learned particulars of her keen eye
which deceives the feigned composure of wet cheeks.

I've discovered new forms of
sovereign disappointment
in the holy manners of God herself
by such agonizingly profound silent emptiness.

I've learned the depth
of what cliches are spoken about
when they want things to go back
to the way they were when it was fun, simple, easy.

I've accepted my capability of
cold violence,
regardless of intentionality or awareness,
when she's counting the weeks since I last held her.

All of these revelations surge over me,
through me like the burden
of a thousand weights that betray
my best wishes for this blissfully happy honeymoon.

One Stable Table

Word vomit of emotion, could be seen as
the stark ravings of a man
seeking discernment,
seeking connection,
seeking purpose.

Doubt.

All the trust I longed to thirst for – courts on high.
We squirm over things like,
experience, tradition, scripture, and reason
to make themes out of the senseless hurt.

Wrestle.

We dance and sing and cry,
write books and attend holy places
all to figure out what we're to do –
why each one of us matters in the stained glass.

Faith.

Perhaps kaleidoscopic vision isn't in line
with dishing out marching orders;
she's giving away all the best vistas for free,
advising us on the way forward.

Love.

Tibetan Practices

Intoxicated breath.
Breath of you, each time.
Coach, come rushing forward
and I'll lead the troops of my heart
toward acquiescence.

Not mine.
Servant of all, this sensual priestess.
Ancient paths provide a song;
inhalation union, this I pray.

Double R

I do not exist.
Fear and trembling.
Embrace infinity today.

Psychology of my mind.
The sociology with community.
Relationships among beings.
Nature relating to itself.

An ecological cure.
Freely giving freely receiving.
This. Here. Now.

Concussive Resonance

Underfoot, already underway.
Reaching into and establishing whole connections,
do not wait for me.

Pieces of a wave blindly existing
which swells tides in and out
with the fluidity of meaning,
sensations of weightless unity:
I the drop, I the crest, I the ocean.

It creates ripples of nostalgia
wherein we relive our memories for stars
to burst and become again –
a drug of captivation.

The Question

The question hits me without rehearsal
and a lifetime of preparation poured out,
in spite of my wayward and lazy preoccupation
with her beauty:

I think it...

Is and was love.
Experience and creativity.
The ground of all being.
Here and now.
Thisness.
The lure and the call forward
toward greater beauty
in every possible, present moment.
The courage to be.
My inspiration.
Captain and cheerleader.
The word and beyond the world.
Self and Sunrise.
My very breath.

...And all other life-giving things.

On A Three-Hour Drive

Dusty.

Deer frightens my path forward through the night while
       technology
fails my many means and yellow ticks endlessly mock me.

Dusty.

What kind of man would I be if I was the one this was saved
       for,
went through pills to prove the passion?

Dusty.

Angels weep for the weakness a boy's trauma can maintain
among mountains of disguise and fortitudinous melancholy.

Dusty.

Wreaking havoc on the binding rope, this highwire act
       knows
no other audience save one, yet fills the entire peninsula for
       kingdom come.

Dusty.

Coffee stains and maple leaves float across the cabin crying
       out
for a moment's notice as I drift too far out of reach.

Dusty does death a disservice;
a loving ache deep into the night.

"Trinity," Padar Island, Indonesia

III.

Haunted & Holy,

or

Life Is Not A Problem To Be Solved But A Reality To Be Experienced

Up & Over

Seeing one final train station table.
Cold and nervous in the snow.
Saving face for the unknown.

Quiet pangs flash,
wet flakes in her melted hair.

Roll out for one last memory.
Windowside and I've wept;
not for goodbyes, but the end.

Rise From Your Tomb

There's serenity to a post-dated grave,
to redeeming the earth's dank coolness
with sweat and smiles, energy and love.

One more laugh, one more kiss.
The flesh returned to these unsung bones
is calling me forever home.

Life after death and there's no other hope but
that of a zeal toward beauty and the very
plausible opportunity of existential zest.

Houdini

Trembling,
like the tear stuck to my eyelid breaks thru rippling rage.

Uncontrollable,
flight appears to win discourse and wet the papyrus of lament.

Pity,
not fear, but for what could be.

Be gone,
riotous escapism, dissolving strangulation,
for I am the way out.

Pontius Pilate's Drinking

Part I: Fading in On a Long March

The fatigued centurion stops in their tracks to rest,
but instead collapses.
Year over year tied together
in decrepit unison while grit grinds to rust,
sunset on any once-held superstition
dipping below the bay's enchantment.
In its place a ruptured chain of succession
finally lurching forward no more,
paralysis an icy bemusement.
Only last calls to savor the cruel genetic taste
of irrelevant lineage
and all-consuming insatiability.

Moments now lost in time,
machinery broken down
to stubs and nothing more,
save for the blood coursing through this singular
       achievement.
A soul held gingerly together
between brisk luminescent hands
forgives itself once more with purposeful resolve.
Permissions anew lead inward where
brick-building sinews exalt virtuously,
their dead weight having since evaporated
across these last few miles.

Part II: A Face Turn for the Ages

The indistinct depths burst forth into song
and what was once absent is suddenly found within.

Through prolific, repopulated participation
a spring erupts eternal.
Wooden beams no longer creak
their distant, graven vows of
an isolated dirge-filled prayer.
The multitudes swim free amongst new expressions
which waters the lands with bucolic abundance.
Patience sustained between few options
as the architecture of suffering's acceptance
is chosen in a perpetual act of defiant worship.

Hope has produced the vivid tapestry of color
adorning these courageous festivities
knowing we've denounced the liquid curse.
Gracious host of a swelling soul is
now unshackled and free to fly.
Like the rich moonbeams inspiring
that intrepid tin ghost along the once weary way,
so too does his fog light shine onward.
Unfettered, the aching dim binds his rapturous heart no
        more.

Part III: My Endearing Sustenance

Because of this,
I have often been hurt.
And for this,
I am no longr apologetic.
Yet by this,
I am now at my utmost gleaming.

King Louie Waterfall

Scarcely cresting one last rocky cliff,
I make a beeline for the pool waters
and fidget with enough patience to play coy
around the idea of diving right in.

So, I do,
cracking my left shin on the shallow stones.
Obligatory photo session aside and completed,
I'm left alone by the distracted pair of foreign lovers.

It takes a moment to find my peace,
I ignore the brief nagging of a leaf or two.
Nearly all of me is submerged below,
leaving room for my lips to usher essence into words
and so that my eyes may commune to witness God.

I can feel it all around me in this rush of divine creation
– my beloved goodness, accepted richness,
strength in glory.
They flow and surge here,
crisscrossing my spirit
like the unseen index of love.

I am unified,
no longer apart from the whole
…and I pray these swirling leaves wouldn't contain such
        prickly corners.

 Vestiges of a Dark Night

Romancing Flavors

Elegance through determination,
she pauses but a second
by the backlit machines
to express gratitude for life's intangibles.

Running upon distant waves' origins,
the warrior poet shames onlookers into wider means,
not through a forced neglect but gleaming radiance.

I sit somewhere off to the peripheral,
yearning to catch a glimpse
of her kaleidoscopic robes,
to melt the ice of what could-be
into fully purposeful
fleshed-out prisms.

Hardships blind those unwilling
to sit and rest
ways which absorb Tonglen airways:
in with fear & out with hope,
in with pain & out with joy,
finding novel pathways toward growing grace.

Still yet still moving,
she wanders divine mystery behind fervent praise
for beings
and energy poised to engage with
at dawn's redemptive side.

Silently, the glow
remains scattered

like the symphonic melodies left behind
and her golden leaves resume
a race already won –
we celebrate its wake,
our victory laps in awe.

Dear Ms. Plath

White nights cajoling her iron army into beckoning arms,
an empty bed pleading for the opportunity to commune.
Kept in close quarters, I sang across endless tales,
ages riling up her seminal pain for a solitary guiding light
to accompany the morose road before me.
Familiar with ever-distant beacons,
being the wiser woman she was,
my advances were gently laid down upon verdant banks.

Prayerful with the muse-like depths of oft-forgotten saints,
she witnessed these muscles ache and
this weary-worn heart through smokey dreams.
Elusive to spontaneously heal such calamity,
these spectral letters of virginal comfort were rather
    misdirected
from the fresh dawn slowly emerging before my very eyes;
unbeknownst to me, my patron flaneur was already guiding
me along with love onto most-blessed holidays.

Elizabeth's Song

You are a windswept spirit
soaring 'cross the golden plains,
reflections of white-puffed majesty dotting oceanic heavens.

You're the throne upon which rests
a cavalcade of compassion,
bouquet of love coursing through the veins
of countless innocent cherubim.

You're the town where I find
pines dreamy enough
to entomb this heart into the ancient songs
passed down in rebirth from founding mothers eternal.

You, whom poets cannot
entrust themselves to express the pastoral essence
of thy nature,
encapsulate all that is
good, true, and beautiful.

For this I bow,
I bend,
I believe.

Meet Your Heroes

Recklessly,
I sought the elusive empress
from such pages of a golden tale
to erase my underground depths
but this too was merely a practice in ego-driven fears.

A man who could ruin his life and an idol-author
behind him were on the sad side for such a love.

Scripted,
she exits stage left.

An experience of one in a transcendent state
as described by poets and mystics –
for a few moments to know true bliss,
a thousand nights of loneliness to despair!

Aren't We All Knights

Sprinting souls pound horizon's pavement
racing toward tomorrow
with unmet hopes in tow.
A brave thrust forward upon the bow of destiny
where more is required than mere chance;
embrace whichever emotions
necessitate the moment's call
diving first beyond fear's unknown
as a singular torchlit flare
illuminates wading waters.

If You Feel Too Much

Every Halloween
I'm faced with specters of the past
from a dreadful night in the ER
which challenged my will
to survive.

October brings haunts
in the form of supernatural monsters
sent to frighten,
yet I persist in hope to battle demons
with such courage
so that they can be endured.

Proudly celebrating
the creepiest time of year,
I've chosen victory
over personal horrors
which cease to relinquish their grip on me.

So, go match
the purest rays of light
screaming for a way out of your
haunted house
and ride home with the warmth of the sun
splashed across your smiling face.

Meet Me At The Gala

We've been patiently hibernating
our entire lives
for precisely this moment
to burst forth in song and dance –

a full parade of butterflies
whistling sweet tunes
just for us
which nary a couple could imagine
skirting but for an instant!

Still, we be the magic makers
of destiny together,
stupefying and mystifying our family friends;
for how else could such
gothic glow of a darkly-fogged
and sanctified coffin-lining
lead me anyplace else besides
my future with you?

Daily Routines

I'm never quite certain of where I am going,
save for the uncanny hope which guides me here
and pushes toward the beyond
with a manic sense of courage.
To be challenged as a shallowed-out leech
with fermenting pride is to expose this
lie of "self" as nothing more
than one atomic perspective gone terribly wrong.

I don't fault myself for these ticks of
weathering and pulsating
beyond most average lengths,
yet astoundingly there's a need
to advance kinetic nature
onto horizons I've barely seen;
where tight-rope harmony develops
my profound sense of
surrender over dread,
rest over despair,
resurrection over a daily death
experienced in endlessly
languid thoughts and exhausting routines.

Could It Be?

Weep together,
my God,
and I will find you
here with me.

Discovered in my beauty,
posited by your hand
as the brushstrokes
circulate affirmations
of presence, of purity,
of forgiven compassion to my core.

The same one
denied under my shoddy,
dogmatic rubble.

If I point to you
demanding healing and a home,
we'll laugh together
at my blind sense
of strained misdirection.

Temporarily Visiting Japan

Remember walking down the hall
and finding yourself warped through
the endlessly-vortexed corridor
of an apartment building you've never known before.
Suddenly, the deeper glow
can begin to reveal desires of the heart:
these stoic crimson and midnight beams
emulating a late-night Kyoto stroll.
In a butterfly's flap,
I'm buzzing beyond the reality of home
and catapulted several thousand miles away –
places I've never been chauffeured through besides in dreams.

Nostalgia cakes the senses,
passed beyond the tunes
of a Tokyo city pop kiss which never was.
But the granted allotment slipped by
like some jolt-triggered truth
where time is twisting itself back into order,
a vapid lack of chaos.
My imagination drifts off to sleep again
as I find the keys to shuffle back into contact with my front
      door.

I've already lost the profound immensity
of that tragically bittersweet moment,
losing every sense of such spotless ecstasy.
Even so, the undulating shockwaves
reverberate from caged ribs
to the cathedrals of my mind
…and that's enough.

Who Are You?

I am dense and expansive in the divine embrace of this soul
by the ever-giving presence of myself, now, here.

The kite, the sky, the water diamonds shimmer,
a flower burning half-dead as the brightest birds do sail.

I am flutes across the dawn and strings of orchestral hope,
broad orchards of love to the famished coves, lost ports, and
            broken harbors.

Not So Lost Causes

If God,
however possibly represented,
meant for some sort of reincarnation
that I'd spend a thousand years
manifested as the rustling pines
along the Pacific coast,
I could see how that's as heaven so intended.

I have professionally become
a karaoke foreigner,
birthing Swift below
my star-studded communist studio
and remembered everything
as I was walking far from home;
a trio of blue books become the
place where the light enters in.

The Return Of Snapshot Memories

Graffitied walls separate cardinals in Berlin,
meditate on the choleric ash of Bangkok mounds.

Asakusa temples entreat Doberman troupes,
to debate the ethics of Lusakan rockabilly.

Dallas to Phoenix is a troubled bridge Simon wrote,
crying rivers into Anhui's paper-lantern town;

Buddha Wat jade shines on the forbidden lens,
toss the slick toothpick into steamy Harajuku ramen.

Rama's dirge lives on in disco-laden tuk-tuks,
awakening worship on Labuan Bajo netted laughter.

Daoshi robes flutter gold like confident bats at night,
held near Bali's holy aggression of naughty macaques.

Vientiane trollies carry new technological marvels,
picked up early in style by Hanoi-chic residual hosts.

Clydesdales prance a frozen jig for me in electrified Harbin,
Cairo sings floating hymns to the tune of its Quran prayers.

The Quiet Life

Tearing up
more at random things -
proof the quiet life can strike a spark in a burdened soul.

To be moved by
love and loss
amidst humanity's excess.

It's all too much…

Still,
I love dancing
when I'm
alone.

Calves Of God (Memories Part 2)

Granny eats snacks
with her Islamic sisters.
Are you Muslim?
I'm honored.
Or a Ukrainian model?
Before dreadful invasions.
A spy seductively asks if I work the shop,
nervously turning down a free lunch.

Kyrie, eleison.
Mr. Mister, Greek for Lord have mercy.
Unquotable, endless War and Peace quotes.
Airport tears taste best with brow's sweat.

Since I am
so young with new money,
who visits ghastly Taoist temples
instead of Sanlitun strip clubs?

Undertaker's truck
in the Flores harbor.
Dilan becomes their famous movie,
celebrating my pinyin name.
Croatia jersey for a global win,
consistent olive branch.

Death of burnt dogs,
Monkeys silently watch,
beached opposite the lapping boat.

More & More

Together
we formed magic
amidst the politically religious,
instant and nameless.

Something I'd lost before,
where upon I recognized significance.

Pretended I let go,
only stirred by a lonely moment of weakness.

Left wanting more,
more she knew I would never have.

If only I'd read the same pages
and could congratulate such mastermind.

No Man's Land

This muscle has burst,
lost in confusion with the head.

Sweat on my brow
and I'm invisible
to myself and no one at all.

Free art up for auction on display.
Flay me from your flags and
I'll make some family proud yet,
O, my bastard soul!

These trenches cannot carry the weight of the world.

Domesticity

I am afraid beyond my years
and passionate fire is only but a weapon
against its owner;
vile trick-of-the-hand halfway through forgiveness,
a reprieve from such foreign, absentee audience.

They dare not hear me
but nevertheless, I extend a hand
toward huddled remains
who have seen worse than civil brutality or faultline
   cleavage.

Hope is all that I have left, no red soldiers.
One by one, a streak down to the floor.
I gave you my all,
fair friends,
and it could never be enough.
Gravity has accepted these bones
a gentle breeze at last.

Afterall

Well, I think today can prove me wrong.
I'll have what it takes to run the light.
And by the end,
barely enough to stand.
Collapse into bedded sheets;
a mess of shuffling feet and empty hands.
Restless, I pass out
into more productive bliss.

Haven't done enough to earn her smile
or make him proud.
Exits fade with each decay
and all resistance
buckles at the constant undertow.

It is the tale of a misled underdog,
that he was ever meant
to fly by conventional means.
Each lifeboat unique
toward a different destination.

Poems, prose, and roses fail,
my monuments erode,
but I'll have
what it takes to succeed.
Just you see.

"Innocence," Victoria Falls, Zambia

Afterword

It would be overly simplistic to say that the months following my health scare went toward healing with increasing ease, but the fact of the matter is that I received better treatment options and eventually found myself in a much more stable condition. It took the adoption of a myriad of physical and mental wellness routines to emerge from places of intense hurt to escape the rock bottom I'd flirted with in the ICU that night. Cliché as it may sound with today's out-in-the-open awareness, but things like diet, social connection, exercise, and spiritual growth all helped garner positive momentum for new, possible directions. In due time, life would develop in wondrous ways as I'd have the fortunate opportunity to travel the world for work, make the most incredible friends, and achieve levels of self-love acceptance that had appeared unfathomable just years prior.

This poetry project had begun just before my "dark night of the soul" and extends far beyond it which is why the collection ranges thematically from those of pained despair to euphoric joy. However, the entire collection revolves around this pivotal spoke of not only maintaining but prioritizing authenticity to one's own self, to one's life experiences, to held beliefs, personal emotions, etc. Times will inevitably change, feelings slowly evolve, and perspectives mature for everyone but amongst it all, I hope that these poems could convey or inspire such sense of transparency, of honesty, of the courage to be true to oneself. At the end of the day this is what I believe matters most by containing the "secret" of discovering an innate, innermost strength to help overcome your lowest lows and then celebrate the highest of highs.

Dylan Podson
January 2024

Acknowledgements

This book has been a labor-of-love, something in the works for over 15 years and so it goes without saying that I could've never accomplished this much without support from a throng of friends and family:

To the Sunset Riders (Mike, Michael, Blayne, Tom), thank you for the childhood any kid could ever dream of with sleepovers and late-night jaunts throughout the neighborhood – you showed me the freedom to feel that I so desperately needed.

To Pat, Kevin, and the Becks, I certainly wouldn't be here today without your brave commitment to this friendship, and I owe you endless praise for the open expression of love that I've received from you all throughout the years of laughter and tribulation.

To my Bible study crew (Chinwe, Kristina, the Graybills, the Sinks), I worked-through so much of this book's themes in your presence (exploring curious discussions) that I'm not sure I could've found such proof of love without your embodied examples.

To Mr. VanWestervelt, the originator of the Vomit Draft, you'll never know how your teaching has inspired and influenced me to become the person I am today – it isn't a stretch to say that this project is only here due to your interpersonal impact.

Finally, to my Mom, Dad, and Sister, you've provided for me in so many direct and unintended ways that I can't imagine a life without your loving embrace to the point that this safety net you've crafted for me became the very womb in which I could be nurtured into an ever-evolving, authentic, beloved self.